Ice Cream, Ice Water, and the Boogeyman

Pamela Bondar

BookLeaf Publishing

India | USA | UK

Ice Cream, Ice Water, and the Boogeyman
© 2024 Pamela Bondar

Presentation by *BookLeaf Publishing*

Web: www.bookleafpub.com

E-mail: info@bookleafpub.com

ISBN: 9789360944148

First Edition 2024

*To anyone fortunate enough to come out on
the other side*

PREFACE

Several years ago, my father unexpectedly passed away. As I processed my grief over his death in therapy, repressed memories of my childhood started to surface. I'd often been amazed at the details of our childhood my sister could recall, while my memories seemed more like the unexplored deep sea. Darkness and pressure suffused my recollection of anything more than some firework shows, bike rides, and swimming pools. As memories bobbed to the surface like buoys lost in a hurricane, I started to recall horrific instances of sexual abuse. Naturally, I figured I must have been misremembering or my brain made false memories. Unfortunately, the further and deeper I got into the healing process, using techniques like EMDR and brainspotting; I started to believe what my memories had shown me. When I underwent a qEEG brain scan, it indicated "Excess slow waves in the back parietal region, and too much theta over the precuneus – suggesting a history of sexual abuse". To me that was the tangible evidence I needed to validate my experience. A pandora's box of pain and processing has been ongoing ever since.

I've seen how deeply this abuse has impacted my life and relationships. While the process of healing has been continuous, and even though I'm secretly crossing my fingers that my mom never reads this, I know the heartbreaking fact is that I'm not alone in my experiences. The collection of poetry within these pages has been a documentation of my journey in realizing the abuse and moving through the days and years beyond it, while also trying to lessen the crushing burden of this knowledge, so I can raise children who will never experience this kind of torment.

I have nothing but respect for those who have been through the worst and come out on the other side causing minimal harm in their wake. If any of these experiences resonate in a painful place in your heart, please know that my heart hurts along with you, and this is not the epitaph of our lives. Unfortunately, trauma happens, and having the strength to reclaim ourselves and move forward is an incredible accomplishment. I'll never stop cheering for you. This book examines difficult topics such as alcoholism, attempted suicide, self-harm, sexual abuse and rape. If you've experienced any type of sexual violence and need help please visit rainn.org or call 1-800-656-4673.

CONTENTS

I Want

I want to be warm inside when it's snowing
I want my nails to be a delicate shape
And pretty colors
I want my hair to be shiny and soft
I want to be beautiful

I want to go to sleep peacefully
I want safe dreams to dance behind my eyes
I want to be cozy
I want to smell nice and unique

I want to have deep conversations
In cozy coffee shops
I want to be handed a free pastry
Because I smiled at the barista and asked about
their day

I want the kindness I put into the world to be
absorbed
And any harm I cause to be forgiven
I want accountability
I want my love to be fully accepted
I want to soak in love
Like sun rays on a beach

I want to shovel my neighbors' sidewalk
I want to leave spare change for the person in
line behind me
I want ripe mangoes and crisp grapes
I want to be creative and quirky and weird

I want my kids to be happy
I want my husband to feel appreciated
I want my sister to feel loved
I want my mom to feel peace

I want kisses and candlelight and romance
I want books and pillows and sexy nightgowns
I want funky useless shit from the thrift store
I want hot showers

I want words that inspire me
To stay in my brain until I can write them down
Instead of being pushed out by song lyrics that
have stayed there for 20 years
I want to be unabashedly myself
I want everyone to be unabashedly themselves

I want the world to be kind
I want ceasefires
And reparations and equity
And the wealth to be distributed
And diseases to be cured
I want anyone who hurts children

To be punished by God
Or the devil for eternity
I don't want my mom to read my poems about
my dad

I want my cat purring
And my dog sighing
Laying together in a strip of sun
On a comfy rug

I want to accept the world for what it is
I want nature to be her relentless self
I want to forgive
I want to be angry
I want humans to be better
I want to be better

Intimacy

Let me care for you
If only it didn't feel
Like dragging a knife down my sternum

Let me open up to you
If only I didn't feel so uncomfortable
Exposing my own viscera

Let me hear you
If only I didn't hear that your every hurt
Was caused by me

Let me choose which is a slower death
Loving someone
Or being loved

I can give love as free and easily as the wind
blows
While I slowly wither with time

But to be loved is to be known
And lobotomizing me would be less painful
Than being fully known

The Dog and the Dishwasher

I could get mad or disgusted
When my dog licks our dirty dishes
While I load the dishwasher
Sometimes I tell her to stop
Shoo her away

Sometimes I pause,
A moment of freudenfreude
Seeing her eyes closed in pleasure
To watch her experience the taste of the
Mashed up black beans on a spoon
Or melted cheese still clinging to the rim of a
plate
With such contentedness
A warmth floods my chest

Does she feel close to me when she tastes what I
tasted?
Does it give her a sense of love and wholeness?
Is it so bad, if I can just run the sanitize cycle
afterwards?

The evidence will be gone
The dishes clean and put away
But she and I will share a memory

Of her happiness
Those closed eyes, the lapping tongue
Enjoying the pleasure
Of my discarded food

And maybe we'll both feel a little more loved

Self Help

c-PTSD
Postpartum Depression
Acupuncture, tinctures, support groups
Talk about it
Don't tell everyone

Al-anon
Talk about your qualifier
It's not your fault
Tell everyone here
Only if you want
Don't tell anyone else
It's anonymous
It's a safe space

Why
WHY
I wish it was different
No one deserves this

Couples therapy
Depression
Books books books
Talk about it
Don't take it personal

It's not personal
It stems from childhood
Don't blame your parents

Grief
Death
Birth
Life
Triggers
Trauma

The Body Keeps The Score
Adult Children of Emotionally Immature Parents
Codependent No More
Self care
Keep talking
Take a break
EMDR
Neurofeedback

It's not personal
It's not your fault
Atomic Habits
You're The One You've Been Waiting For
Work together
Take time
Accountability
Forgiveness
Breathing exercises

Yoga

Keep reading
Keep breathing
It's not linear
Break cycles
Be better
Know better
Do better
DO BETTER
BE BETTER

Time
Time
Time
Time

Eventually will it get better
It will get better
It gets better
Hang on
Hold fast
Trust the process

Healing
Healthier
Helpful
Hope

The Darkness

Today I woke up
My eyes stung with emotion
And shone with resolve
It was time
Time to tell my truth

It is big and dark and scary
A pandora's box of horrors
A sickening sludge that has buried itself
Deep within my chest
Holding all the shame
And pain
And anger
And betrayal

But
I read something to the effect of
"Where pain meets truth comes art"
I can make art
I can tell the truth

Somehow it was communicated with me
That if I ever told
One of us would die
And the evidence was there

I was held down in the darkness
Withheld from air and light
Under his crushing weight
Struggling to breathe
Struggling to live
He let me live
Perhaps he did that to me to prove
That if I said something one of us would die

In the scary, cluttered basement room
Where I'd have to go sometimes to relight the
pilot light
He was there and so was a noose
And he was struggling to live
And I helped him live
Pushing a chair or maybe it was a box under him
so his feet could touch
I was maybe seven years old
He told me he was just fixing something and got
stuck

I saved his life
And he still came into my room
And touched me and made me touch him
And covered me in his weight
And repulsed me with his smell

He'd pour me cereal

Heat me up soup
Prank me and laugh
His eyes never betraying ignorance
Making me question reality

Making my brain store it where it couldn't reach
me
Until one of us died
And I saved his life once
And I believe most of his life
He spent trying to forget
What he'd been doing to me
Maybe repeating something
That had been done to him
But that I'll never know

And I saved his life once
And he died anyway
Many years later, of course
Drunk and alone
And I cried for him

I took the truth
Released the death that no longer threatened me
I turned it into art
Because otherwise it might have killed me

Loving

Loving myself
By writing my poems
Because my experiences can't wither me away
Into nothing
I'm more than that

Loving myself
Drawing my little pictures
Grabbing a little treat
Giving my pain a voice
Sculpting little figures
Taking walks in nice weather
Lizzard time in the sun

Loving myself
By loving my kids
Subtle kisses
On milky cheeks
As their breaths soften with sleep
Keeping them safe
Giving them love

Loving my kiddos
By using their made up words
Speaking in gremlin voices

Disco ball dance parties
Charades and laser tag in the living room
Favorite meals and snacks
Movies and snuggles and nose boops
Protecting them

Loving myself
By giving my love
Because my love is so beautiful
My love is so big
My love is so me

It's so me
And I love
Singing songs about what the dog is doing
Sobbing the words to songs
I've cried to a thousand times
Feeling life
Being myself
I love loving

My Good Brain

My good brain
She protected me from you

The moment you left the room she blocked out
the memory
The betrayal of what had just happened
Time and time again

She taught me to repress, forget

Lest I stick needles in my arms my entire life
To numb what you've done

She made me forget all the trauma
Much of my childhood, too

To protect me from you
To protect me from myself

Lest I swallow a bottle of pills to end the shame,
suffering, and guilt that would've riddled me
Because I would have believed it was my fault
You would have let me believe it was my fault

If I'd remembered what you did to me

All my nights would have felt unsafe
All my days would be haunted by you

You should've been my protector

But you weren't

So she did it
She tried so hard

She kept everyone at an arm's length
Leaned into being an object to others
Because she was sexualized before her breasts
had budded
Before blood stained her clothes brown
And there was comfort in the familiar
It makes a lot of sense now
As I grew up
Why I had to be drunk to have sex with anyone

She kept me safe

Lest I drag knives up and down my flesh
Because I couldn't explain the pain I was in
So I'd create my own
Just to know it was real

It should've been you
In pain

Lonely
Betrayed

Perhaps compassionate me would know that you were
But now my good brain feels righteous anger

Now my good brain is learning out of her old habits
That kept me safe
Because I realize it's no longer serving me

Lest I become someone that drinks herself to death
Like you did

Even my good brain in her righteous anger
Won't go so far to say you deserved it
But she will scream
And shout

That I deserved better.

14-17

Walking in sleeting wind
7 deep across the road
4 boys and 3 girls
My knock off Jncos
Soaking up freezing muddy gutter water
Feet frozen, ears red and throbbing
But I felt like I belonged
4 o'clock in the afternoon

Listening to Green Day
Social Distortion
Bad Religion
Eminem
Scream Singing lyrics down the street
Laughing so much it hurt

Riding the local bus, Transfort
Stealing vodka from the freezer
And replacing it with water
1 o'clock in the morning
Leaving out of my bedroom window

The CSU college guys
Giving us weed and beer
Expected something in return

And eventually took it without asking
But I just
Hit my head and went to lay down
But woke up undressed and disoriented

I remember what I was wearing
A light pink sweater
A white studded belt
Light jeans
I had braces

Walking the streets
3 o'clock in the morning
Still a kid
This time alone
This time dry
But still frozen
Crying so much it hurt
Where were my friends now
And why don't I belong anymore

A brave friend of mine asked me
To persecute the guy named Fred
Who had done to her what he'd done to me
At 17 I was too scared
For my parents to know
To admit it aloud again
To be forever tethered to it
Too scared

For justice to be served

As an adult I have to forgive my teenage self for
that

Cleansing

One morning I sat in the sun
I let smoke from Palo Santo cleanse gemstones
that normally sit beside my bed
She snaked around the stones
Opaque yet translucent
And promised to lift away the negative energy
absorbed by them
To cleanse
To cleanse
To cleanse

I let the smoke linger
Secretly hoping it would cleanse me too
My unsteady hands that are tired
From holding on to pain with clenched fists
Imprinting crescents from fingernails into my
palms
I can still smell her citrus scent clinging to my
acrylic nails
My shaky voice that's often drowned by doubt
and fear
Too stifled to manifest the life I want
Too unsure about sending my truth out to the
world
Too cowardly to give it words

I can taste her woodsy depth on my tongue, after
I breathed deep her smoke
Deep into the little girl I hold in my heart
I feel a spark

She wishes the smoke would cleanse the stones
she carries
They are filled with pain
With fear
With loneliness
With abandonment
With confusion

I promised her I'd try to cleanse them
(only to later realize cleansing them wasn't my
task)
But instead she and I went on adventures
Found a beautiful forest
An immaculate greenhouse belonging to a queen
We made an ornate box of stones, gems and
precious metals.

I squeezed her tight to me and we placed our
stones inside
Because they're too powerful for me to cleanse
(the unspoken truth is they're still too scary to
hold)
I won't lie to her, she knows
She knows I'll return

Sometimes to add stones
Examine stones
Shout and cry at the stones
I don't understand how the stones work, but I
know the power they hold

We know magic won't cleanse them
But we still wish it would
Because they're so heavy
They are stones after all
They weigh us down
Down
Down
Down

So far down all we see is darkness
All we feel is pressure
All we taste is bitterness
And we're lonely
She and I

But I'm the adult now
I hold her (I'm present with you, honey)
Reassure her (no need to fear with me, my love)
Squeeze her hand (I'm here with you,
sweetheart)
Stroke her hair (I won't leave you, darling)
She never had that before

She cried, shook, screamed
She put down the stones
The smoke curled around them
Cleansing
Cleansing
Cleansing

I secretly hoped the smoke would cleanse me
too

Peace

I can find peace
In the sunlight that streams through windows
On the soft velvet ears of cats and dogs
In the long dark eyelashes of my children
I can find peace

I can breathe deep
When I remind myself to stand tall
To look up
Take in the sky
Take in the stars
I can breathe deep

I can send love
On the wind
With my hands
To the parts of me
That never felt like enough
I can send love

I can grieve
In my words
On my face
With all my heart
I can grieve

I can heal
One day at a time
With my peace
With my breath
With my love
With my grief
I can heal

The Love My Parents Had

I didn't want the type of love my parents had
Truth be told, I didn't remember seeing it
What I saw was pain and bitterness
Like exhausted fighters throwing the last of their
jabs
Waiting for the bell that would never ring
Never being relieved of their pain
Never loving through their pain

I was 30 when I realized they had truly loved
each other
My father's cold body lay on a steel table
My mother cradled his head and kissed him
The most tender thing I'd ever seen

A life of theirs flashed before my eyes
They were so happy
So full of love and meant for each other
It was beautiful and crushing in the 2 seconds it
took to see
25 years of love that never happened

My mother let her golden love shine
My father didn't use the guise of night to hurt
me

Instead I saw them

Dancing in the kitchen
Familiar linoleum beneath their feet
Sharing spatulas to lick batter from
Staying awake late in the blue light of the TV
Holding hands

Days and nights brightened and faded
Fights ended and resolved
They grew together
In wholeness
In love

Time passed, I grew up a child of love
Became a full adult capable of love
Of wholeness
Grown into who I should've been

Their hands withered and wrinkled in unison
Their gray hair mirrored in their graying eyes
Their words slowed
And their voices softened
Like the crinkled tissue paper the skin around
their eyes had become

My father didn't die, drunk and estranged
My mother didn't surround herself with silence
and eggshells

It was a beautiful fantasy
It was a painful reminder of reality
How hard I've had to work to become more
Than the product of parents who couldn't love
through their pain
They did their best
Now I'm trying my best
To love and be loved

I don't want our kids to have the love we had
When I almost let pain destroy us
Because I'm not their pain
I have my own, and you have yours
Thank God we're trying to love each other
through it
So our kids can look back
And want the kind of love their parents had

Untitled

A blockade
A barrier
The unreliable narrator

Abandoned
Abused
Gaslit
Used

Discarded
Betrayed
Brokenhearted
Disobeyed

Angry
Unruly
Stoic
Unsturdy

Defiant
Determined
Rebellious
Unburdened

Creative

Empathetic
Courteous
Playing catch up

Smart
Funny
Underestimated
Sunny

Charming
Agreeable
Brave
Reliable

Authentic
Courageous
Resourceful
Loquacious

An open gate
A way through
A trusted heart
A life, anew

Ice Cream, Ice Water, and the Boogeyman

Girlhood to womanhood
A stumbling journey
Something always got misplaced
Something always got stolen
Jewelry from Claire's in the mall
A favorite sweater or CD
Innocence

I remember the feeling of having ice water
Dumped on me while I showered
Howls of laughter drowned my startled
screeches
I remember the feeling of drinking ice water
After eating soft serve ice cream
Drinking it down
Somehow crisper and more refreshing than it's
ever been
Or ever will be again
The feeling of spinning until I fell
Dizzy in the front yard
The hopeful ignorance
Of not knowing if anyone has a boogeyman
Like mine

I always wondered why it felt like
Nobody knew me
Turns out I didn't get a chance to know myself
I was stolen before I could form
I died quietly when the nightly visits from the
boogeyman started
Withered on the floor
Of my childhood bedroom
White walls with pink trim
My favorite ruffled pillowcase
And the girlhood that never had a chance to be

I grew into a woman I never fully knew
Recapitulating the familiarity I found in my
trauma
Binge drinking
Disordered eating
Migraines
Anxiety and panic attacks
Hangovers that stole days away
Girlhood gone and forgotten

Somehow I feel numb and heartbroken all the
time
Disassociating
Distracted
Soundlessly sobbing in closed cars and on
steam-filled shower floors
Words describing the agony

Washed down the drain
Mourning me
Mourning her
My precious girlhood who never had a chance to
grow

Giving her pieces of girlhood at the cusp of forty
Sounds as ridiculous as it feels
But not as ridiculous as not knowing
The full grown woman
Who looks back at me in the mirror

Whittled

I let myself get whittled down
My therapist says it was how I survived
That I didn't have a choice
She said it was actually brilliant of little me
I found the ways they'd let me fit
And let them whittle me into shape

Shave off that parts that were too much
Too talkative
Too loud
Too nosy
Too needy
Too selfish
Always so selfish

In adulthood I realized
Having basic needs
Isn't selfish

I'll say that again
Having basic needs
Especially as a child
Isn't selfish

The fact that that has to be a revelation

Is heartbreaking

I want to tell that little girl
The one who felt like such a burden
Like such a bother
Like she was stupid
That they failed her
They didn't mean to
Of course
They did their best
But she suffered
Even with their best

She suffered

Almost 40

Nightly ginger lemon tea sits beside my bed
Gray streaks in my hair
Wrinkles in the mirror
When did I get this fucking old?

This isn't even old
Unless you ask
Hollywood,
Instagram,
Or my children

Knee pain
Adhesive Capsulitis
Mammograms
Sure does feel fucking old

Nostalgia gets me
Even when I know it's a marketing tactic
But I'm damn susceptible to it
Hell yes Dr. Dre as the halftime show sponsored
by beers I don't let myself drink

I actually love the younger generations
The slang is fun
The way they romanticize the years of my youth

Makes me look at it in a different light
Even if they see me as old and lame
So what if I am

Getting older isn't horrible
I mean, I'm too cheap for botox
So I cut my own bangs in the mirror
Too cheap to see a stylist :::shrug:::

I lived through this messy amazing life
All the love
All the tiny deaths of my former selves
All the lessons
And their daggers through my heart

I give less shits with age
And that's so freeing
With age comes less people-pleasing
Another death of a former self
I thank her
And appreciate having outgrown her

On to the new
On to getting older
Moving with time
Which moves fast as fuck
For such an old bitch

The Apple Falls

My grandpa smelled like sawdust, machine
parts, and Irish Spring soap
He spoke with humor of his friends
At a job from which he'd long been retired
He'd gently share the blurry edges of serving
during a war
Assuredly and expertly avoiding the trauma and
grief

He'd reread us stories from the same books
So many times
I was an adult before I realized
He must've had them memorized for years
He spilled his iced tea at the dinner table so
many times
It became a long-running family joke
I held his hand as his exhale stopped asking for
an inhale in return

My grandmother was a dutiful wife
She prepared every meal, our favorites every
single time we visited
Baked cookies and breads and cakes for us to
enjoy after each meal

Scooped us bowls of cold, sweet ice cream
drizzled in sticky chocolate syrup
Before bed when we would sleep over
She sat patiently as the conversations flowed
around her
She still does that

She says she's relieved she has no one to cook
for
Under those fluorescent kitchen lights
On that cold hard tile floor
Though the shine in her eyes suggests different
She too, expertly and assuredly avoids sharing
grief and trauma
Except when
Her tiny frame crumpled as she wailed when I
had to tell her
That her son was gone

As a child
I used to wonder why my dad was so sad
His parents were the nicest people I've known
He'd never served in a war
I only knew he was sad because
He'd let tears fall after the recycling bin was full
to the brim with silver cans
As an adult
I wonder if it was guilt or grief for what he'd
done

Each time he slipped into my room after
midnight

I tried to be a dutiful child
Always reading the unspoken words on the faces
around me
So many times
I was an adult before I realized I'd memorized
them all
The expressions and exhales that signaled
danger to me
Teaching myself the instinct of hyper-vigilance
Knowing my needs needn't exist
Not knowing I'd been abandoned
But feeling a profound loneliness I couldn't
express
My brain expertly and assuredly avoiding
Any understanding of the trauma I was
withstanding
Until the grief came

When the threat of him died along with him
With time and EMDR
I could finally decipher the clouded canyons my
mind wouldn't visit
And I have no way to avoid the grief and trauma
any more
It scratches and claws its way out of me

Sometimes erupting from me in sobs and
screams
Other times it quietly paralyzes my very will to
exist
I have no choice but to break the cycle of
avoidance
It has no right to live forever within me
When I'll eventually die
When everything else dies

As I slowly bleed out the pain
Bravery is replacing the trauma
The grief still sits on my chest
And sometimes runs achingly down my arms
But it's pushing me to send the pain away
If it lives in me it will fester, become hurt I
instill into others
My children will not become full time
shareholders in my pain, trauma, and grief
Which is why it must painstakingly live and die
on these pages instead

My Father's Eyes

I've been complimented endlessly
On my hazel eyes

His eyes were hazel too
He breathed shaky, beer-soaked breaths
Into my ear
While I pretended to sleep
Closing tight my hazel eyes

And my eyes are like his eyes
My eyes are beautiful
My vision imperfect

His eyes were blurred
In sight and morality
I don't remember his eyes as beautiful
They looked foggy to me

Their gaze made me nauseated
If I looked into them too long
I'd taste bile
Smell the alcohol seeping from his pores
Feel his grip, unyielding on my innocence

My eyes are like his eyes
But I love my eyes

They contain galaxies
His contained secrets
Saw double

If I think about him
And how my eyes are like his eyes
I'll want to gouge mine out
Because it's the last of him I can purge
From my life
He ignored the part in the Bible
That told him to cut out
That which causes him to sin
Or he'd had no hazel eyes
And no rights to mine

I decided he no longer gets to cause me harm
And my eyes are like so many eyes
That aren't his
His eyes are ash now
Buried and gone

My eyes are vibrant
Spilling secrets
Sharing love and sparkles
Flowing freely with truth and tears

His eyes never look back at me in the mirror
They aren't his eyes
They're just mine

Tired

I'm tired of myself
Of my little poems
Complaining about my trauma
Complaining about my parents
Complaining
Complaining
Complaining

Like what now,
Does my shit magically fix itself
I feel like I've said all I need to say…
I'm better at communicating
I'm better at voicing my wants and needs
I guess I could be better at having boundaries…
I can take care of myself

I know there are dark pits
With the hardest stuff to face
Stuff too difficult to put into words
Let alone a silly little poem

After the sludge is cleared
(does it clear?)
Then what do I write about
I'm not good at nature and love poems

All I know to write is pain
What happens when it's not connected to me
like a shadow?

Will I rest?
Will I dance?
Will I be free?
Will I still be me?

8/22

I brought you back to life today
Reading old texts between us
You texted exactly like you spoke
Shallow
Short
Sometimes unintelligibly

It's been long enough
Seven years today
You used to swing me by my ankles
Screeching
In our front yard
Then, dizzily
I'd chase hummingbird moths
From our flowers

I loved you

The few memories of childhood I hold are now
soured
By what you did
I was a little girl who loved her dad so much
She didn't understand how you were also
The boogeyman

She could have died along with you
I almost let her
That's how angry I am
I'd kill a part of me to get rid
Of the pain you caused

But I know better
I'm nurturing that part of me now

The little girl who loved you sleeps peacefully
No shadows lurking in her room
There is no threat of her bed
Creaking under your weight
Your liquor-soaked breath
Won't suffocate her anymore

And still
Every now and then
The little girl who loved you
Brings you back to life

Jump

Somewhere along the line
Carved by the roots of the family trees
That joined together and split apart
Somebody got hurt
Somebody hurt somebody

The pain ricocheted
Throughout decades
Maybe centuries
It touched every strand of DNA
Passed along like a birthmark

It landed in my bedroom
And swallowed me into an abyss
Dark
Unyielding
All-encompassing

The pain of fathers and mothers
Sisters
Cousins
It landed on us all
A continuous cycle
Gripping generations
Like tree roots gripping the earth beneath them

I watched my family
Struggle with it
In their own ways
Avoidance
Numbing
Recapitulating

Eventually
I recklessly stood at the edge of a cliff
My choices carved into my lineage
Follow follow follow
The path is already there
Do what they all did, have done, and will do
again
Or
Jump

I jumped
I jumped to break the cycles
I jumped to break free
I jumped
And landing in a different place fucking hurt
But not as much as it'd hurt
To see my kids inherit my pain

Always

There have been times
When I convinced myself
I'd fallen out of love with you
And back in
In and out
Up and down
Down
Until I drowned
Tore everything to the ground
Burned it to ash
Never intending to rebuild it

I fell in love
Again
With you
My broken heart
My broken mind
My broken body

Won't stop loving you

Your plan was always to rebuild
To never let go
But the way you dealt with your pain
Hurt me too

So my plan was to swim
As far away from the shore as possible
Hoping to disappear on the horizon
But I kept drifting back
Cresting the surface
One breath away from my last
It hurt you, me wanting to swim away
For that I'm so sorry, my love

I'm not used to writing love poems
But you dried my hair
You saw my broken pieces as whole parts of me
You stayed
You fought
You burned with me
Always intending to rebuild

Knowing it was always me
For you
Realizing it wasn't just me
Needing to rebuild
You worked for me, for you
Towards me, towards us
Always

And that made me want to
Write you a love poem